TH
AND THE

by Michael Robinson

Martin House Publishing, Keene, Ontario K0L 2G0   (705) 295-4491

Martin House Publishing wishes to thank
Mary Lou Fox, Marianne Hogbin and Linda Zernask
for their encouragement and advice in the production
of this book.

First printing: April 1991
Second printing: September 1991
Third printing: August 1993

Designed and printed by Commercial Press, Peterborough, Ontario

Canadian Cataloguing in Publication Data

Robinson, Michael, 1948 -
  The earth and the dancing man

Poems and drawings.
ISBN No. 0-9695225-0-9

1. Indians of North America - Poetry. I. Title.

PS8587.0356327 1991   C811'.54   C91-093985-3
PR9199.3.R628327 1991

Martin House Publishing, R.R. 1, Keene, Ontario K0L 2G0   (705) 295-4491

Dedicated to William N. Graburn
1903 - 1989

ILLUSTRATIONS

Page

Walking Between Two Worlds 16

The Fourth Hunter 20

The Earth and the Fifth Child 24

Looking For America 28

The Last Days of Promise 34

Dreaming in a Rolling Wind 38

Places With No Names 42

The Flute Player 46

Stone Garden 50

A Blind Man's Rush Into the Sky 54

The Danger of Power 58

Life on the Moon 62

Living Inside a Child's Dream 66

The Witness 70

A Shadow of a Bird 74

CONTENTS

Page

Introduction 6

The Earth and the Dancing Man 8

Water 14

Walking Between Two Worlds 17

The River 18

The Fourth Hunter 21

The Earth and the Fifth Child 25

Looking For America 29

A Hermit's Prayer 32

The Last Days of Promise 35

Dreaming in a Rolling Wind 39

Places With No Names 43

The Flute Player 47

Stone Garden 51

A Blind Man's Rush Into the Sky 55

The Danger of Power 59

Life on the Moon 63

Living Inside a Child's Dream 67

Children of Fire 68

The Witness 71

New World Order 72

A Shadow of a Bird 75

Epilogue 77

Prophecy of Movement 78

INTRODUCTION

T here lives in all of us a very private, precious entity which we perceive to be a 'spirit' of some kind, to which all religion and mysticism addresses itself in an effort to dialogue with this 'other', in an attempt to find our place in the myriad conjunctions that define our universe. Poetry is a way of speaking to souls. It is at once direct and cyclical and illuminates its own truths for those that would venture into the unlit areas of our being. The power of poetry then, would be in its unique ability to speak to us in its own 'parallel' language addressed to our 'parallel' selves.

The power and strange beauty of Michael Robinson's poems seem to reside in the ability to penetrate the mundane reality of the visible world and join it with the unseen twin of its own being, permitting us to feel, for a moment, the unrestricted sense of timelessness in which he pairs the two halves that constitute the mystery and gift of our being.

Carl Beam
Peterborough, Ontario
April 2, 1991

Where there is no wilderness
There is no God.

THE EARTH
AND THE DANCING MAN

T he man by the lake
was forced to live forever.
The man was afraid of living
forever,
but fear and greed
had grabbed him at the same time
and flung him away.

He had spent his entire life
seeking the idea of freedom.
Freedom of death, from fear
or freedom from life,
by searching for the door to eternity.
His quest cost him everything.

The search finally brought him
to a lonely hill, overlooking
a small pond.
He stood there, facing the west wind
as it slowly blew him away.
Piece by piece.
Like bits of bark
or pages from a discarded book.

When the wind died away
there was nothing left
of his quest,
of his years of struggle...

He suddenly realized
he was standing *in* the pond.
Totally bewildered and soaking wet.
The man quickly looked around,
then looked up
at the hill behind him.
The hill... he remembered standing on the hill.
It was the last and the only thing
he could remember.
He had no memory of leaving the hill
or entering the pond.
The man's eyes turned back
and stared at his hands
just below the surface of the water.
Something was very wrong...?
very different.
Something was gone.
He was the same man
yet he was not.
He wondered why he felt
no fear
or perhaps regret.

He did feel alone,
very much alone and hollow;
yet he knew that this hollow
place within him
was probably the only place
that was really him.
He was totally empty.
Separate and a stranger,
like a small bird
in a world of no birds.

He was also filled with a sudden
realization that although he still
breathed and could see the world,
he was now on the outside
of life.

Years ago he was told it would be hard to "cross over",
a lifetime and more of learning.
The journey would happen fast
but it would be very hard,
and almost impossible to return
especially if he travelled alone.
No words or stories
would or could prepare
the traveller
for what lay ahead,
whether eternity would be heaven
or hell.

Whether this choice would be just
a handful of sand
or an endless desert.
A new life
or an old death,
or something in between.
He felt a great disappointment
that the world around him,
looked the same
as it had before.
He had allowed himself
to fantasize what it might be like.
That had been a mistake.

Sitting alone in the water
he felt no cold,
only wet.
Gone, blown away,
were all his human feelings,
his human reactions
to the elements around him.
To himself.

Slowly the man returned
to the small hill top.
There he sat for a long time
looking over the pond,
not seeing the water
or the sky.
A horrible thought occurred
to him.
He was lost.
He had somehow missed
the window.
He was trapped somewhere
at the edge of life.
Life as he had known it...
had left it.
So close yet so far away
from the black window
to freedom,
from the paradise of his own imagination.
He should not have come
alone.
He had allowed his ego to be his strength
not his heart.
That too,
was a mistake.

If he was human,
he would have cried out
in despair.
If he was human,
he would have cursed himself.
Killed himself,
abandoning all sense of control.
But he was no longer a man.
So all he could do
was watch
and wait.

Suddenly the sky in front of him
split open with a loud snap,
revealing a narrow silver doorway.
It sparkled and shimmered, as though it was alive.
Something danced out
and touched his eyes,
then raced back.
It seemed to call to him,
beckoning him to come;
to leave the hill.
But the man was numbed
by disbelief at what he saw
and frozen by utter fear.
He could not speak,
but only stare.
At the moment of truth
he was suddenly without any.

Like a leaf on a tree
that could not leave
the branch,
he was now more dead
than alive.
Stuck to his fantasy
of paradise.
He had now become the
ultimate truth
of his own vanity.

A king
with no servants,
no kingdom,
no sword or gold.
And no claim to his own
existence...
lingering forever
on the threshold of an idea,
living forever
with his own fear...
looking through the door to eternity.

WATER

The earth never offered man
Water
As a gift

Water was part of her
It is her blood
Her moving force

And in this, she said
You will see your greed
Your mistakes
Your image
But few will see me.

Walking Between Two Worlds

WALKING
BETWEEN TWO WORLDS

Walking between two worlds
is on a battle ground of fear,
logic and the illusions of distance
and of crippling cold.
It is a kingdom of dreams,
(a place to pass through them... to survive.)
It is the distance between real and forever
and death.
And here, death is the King,
a twirling dancing warrior,
a piece of black smoke, grinning... waiting.
It is the only thing in life
that waits for man.

The day had stopped.
The sun, a dim grey ball,
is frozen solid.
It cannot move and the rolling snowy landscape
taunts me and calls me to hurry on,
as its spirit darts this way and that,
laughing, as though it were all a game.
The cold wastes no time on the dying.
It watches me, like a solitary figure on a hill top.
I cannot see its face,
yet it seems to be waiting.
I know I cannot stop.
Each step I take, is a loud crunch, a splitting crack.
The sound never stops.
And it's the only sound I can hear.

THE RIVER

Man's endless quest
to discover and control
his own destiny,
is like a frightened child
racing down a torrent river.

The truth of destiny,
is the river itself.

The Fourth Hunter

THE FOURTH HUNTER

The first hunter disappeared
into the eyes of the bird he killed,
becoming a circle of light,
turning, falling forever.
He never knew the difference.

The second hunter became lost
in a mist
at the edge of a deep lake.
When suddenly the past
and the future
raced in together like giant fingers,
splitting him into two halves.
His left side stumbled
and fell into the water.
His right side was unaware
that the left side was gone.

The third hunter
made a huge mirror
and began singing as loud
as he could,
to his reflected image.
He slowly turned to stone
to hide his sorrow and apathy.
You can still hear him singing.

The fourth hunter
who discovered how to make
fire
in a dream,
sat alone on a high hill.
Below him,
the world spread out
forever
like a river; an ancient turtle, within a living shell.

Far into the distance,
Infinity awaits...
like a small bird.
Its eyes, a window.
Its spirit,
on fire.

The Earth and the Fifth Child

THE EARTH
AND THE FIFTH CHILD

The thin line between reality and infinity
is a doorway
no one can see.
A small beetle
hiding among the rocks.
A window that is more a mirror
and shadows,
than a passage way of light.

The thin line of secrets
has no reality.
No sense of touch, or time.
The line is in perfect balance.
It is pure movement,
on the edge of man's ability
to grasp
and understand
what is around him.

Men, lost on vision quests,
men looking for the face of God,
looked up
and saw the earth
drifting along,
far out in space.

They fell to their knees
and touched the ground
beneath their feet.
It was cool and lifeless.
They knew, as they had been told,
that the light was divine,
the soul of the history
of the earth.
But they had no idea
what it really was,
what it looked like.

Four of the lost men
died lonely deaths
sitting dumbfounded,
empty.
Staring up at the drifting earth.
The fifth man
lost his ability to reason
and ran blindly into the rocky hills,
running through an invisible
fog.
He disappeared.
He was now free, beyond the gate.

The fifth child
is born of no design.
No plan.
He waits just beyond the earth.
He waits to be born,
to be seen.
He is a thin line of light
turning slowly
circling silently, in dark space.

Looking For America

LOOKING FOR AMERICA

L ooking for America
was the searching for the fourth circle.
Now it is the search for the fifth circle.
A continuing quest left behind
by ancient Prophets,
left behind in stone circles
to mark the way,
never telling
where the path goes
or ends.
The horizon is alive
and races along,
never stopping, never waiting
and never giving rest
to those who follow it.

It is the path
where hunters are hunted.
Where looking can blind you.

It is a path
of alien landscapes
and laughing spirits
that dart in and out,
racing along the rolling hill tops,
calling out to weary travellers
who have become
more like shadows
than men.

It is a journey of ghosts,
who whisper names at night,
hiding in places of shadows
and silence.
They make warriors, prisoners...
in their sleep
and children in the day.

America is a place of ancient spirits
lying in wait...
within walls of stones,
separating men in two halves,
like a canyon with no bottom
or heart.
America is the stranger
calling out from distant hills.
The echo of history.
The lonely man with no face.
The inventor of fire
and the drum.

As the weary hunter
finally looks out,
across the last river valley,
he sees America.
But he is no longer free.
The hunter realizes
he is the stranger
on the hilltop.

He is the stone.
He is alive.
And he knows this path
will never end.

The hunter can never stop.
Beyond the valley
is the fifth house.

"America" does not mean U.S.A.
It is the name for this continent
in the time when the spirit of
the wilderness was silent and virgin,
untouched by cold hands,
alien to fear and profit.

America was a unique 'stone garden'
that grew and nurtured life
and her children,
in a never ending dream.

A HERMIT'S PRAYER

I looked up
and saw the Earth
drifting,
drifting.

I looked in
and saw my spirit
crying,
crying.

I looked down
and saw my shadow
watching me.

The Last Days of Promise

THE LAST DAYS OF PROMISE

History and the future
are abstracts
that cocoon the realization
of the moment.
The abstract is the movement
that sustains life...
that identifies life
from other ideas of reality
and protects the beauty
of its spirit.

Beyond the abstracts
lies a pitch black
titanic rolling entity,
so vast, so dense and silent
so completely alien,
that the reality of past and future
could not exist.
The movement
that is called life
would disappear forever.

The universe rolls on
and on
and the fragile light
of man
is hard to see,
and is lost,
in the huge shadow
that follows.

The promise
that life would continue
and follow this light,
is held in secret
by ancient Pipe Women.
But it too,
is being turned
and blown away.

Yesterday I looked
and saw a fifth woman.
A fifth singer.
A cold chill ran
up my back.
The new woman
was the only one singing.

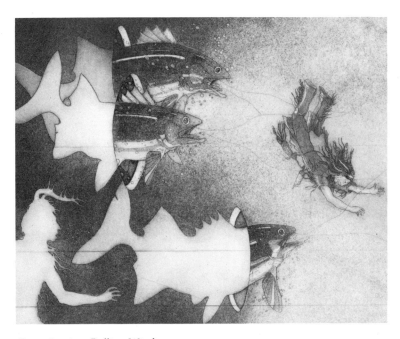

Dreaming in a Rolling Wind

DREAMING IN A ROLLING WIND

The shadow man.
The shadow of the invisible man
is the door into the unknown.
His dream is thunder,
like huge wings
pounding the ground.
And his eyes...
His eyes are the fear
that holds the dream
and the dreamer
as two spirits, strangers
on a single path.

The shadow of the man
is his dream.
The doorway is a movement,
a flicker in the night,
a small dark hole
like a black moth, with no eyes.
and then the man's shadow is gone.

The dream is now alive, real
racing madly through a tunnel...
colours, noises, and bits of light
trail behind like a swirling, glittering, smoky snake.
Suddenly the roles have changed.
The dream is the dreamer
and the dreamer is a shadow,
an alien bird, free
in an invisible sky.
Free,
in a dance of life,
in a dance of death.

Places With No Names*

PLACES WITH NO NAMES

Somewhere on the west coast of
South America,
there was a small cave.
In the darkness of the cave,
there was a silence,
like a secret, hidden away
from profit or greed.
It had rolling eyes
and the wisdom to wipe out all life.
It was the final balance
between the past and the future.
Between life and death.
It waited like the written word.
In its right hand, was the spirit.
In its left hand, was the smoke.
The cave faced west.
This is the direction the silence
blows.

The cave was the passage way
between worlds without names.
They are places of power.
They are placed to wait.
The cave was a place
where we were born
and a place from where
we will leave.

A cave was a lost time
and a place to hide
history.
But the cave was no place
for kings
and men with black hats.

* This print is to honour such a cave. A place that was stolen and used as a dump. Finally it was dynamited. Blown away.

The Flute Player

THE FLUTE PLAYER

There was a man, a flute player,
who heard the bird-like music
at a time when there were
no seasons.
No one else heard it,
though many people were there
and have spent days since,
waiting and listening
from the top
on Old Man's hill.

The night the flute player died,
they could hear a flute playing
from the hill.
No one dared
to go back on the hill.
The flute was never found.
A veil of fear,
like a mist,
settled over the entire hill top.

The fear was sacred.

The world around the hill
began to slowly
blow away...
piece by piece.
First the birds left.
Then the people lost
their ability to dream.
Soon they lost their hearts,
then their children
disappeared.
Next the trees turned to shadows.
The water became stone
and crumbled in agony.

The world was dying
in a mist of dust.
There was nothing left
except fear,
silence and nowhere to hide.

Blindness became the spirit
of the living.

The secret of the music
will be lost forever,
until the flute can be found.
Until the strange bird singers
are heard again.
Until someone rediscovers
the music
hidden in the Earth
on Old Man's hill.

Stone Garden

STONE GARDEN

The old man society
is a society of Hermits,
Prophets without names.
A thousand small caves,
in a thousand hillsides,
in a thousand swirling dreams,
moving to the click
of the dream sticks.
click.
click.
click.
click.
A monster in the eyes
of the blind.
A ghost to those
who wait by the water.
To the dreamers it is
a reflection,
a mirror image
of their own souls.

To the old men,
the clicking is a hollow ancient
sound.
A heart beating
that never stops.

The old men wait
inside the garden
and watch
the race
between eternity and kings.
Flashes of light,
like crazy night birds
going around and around and around.

The stone garden
is all there is.

All there was.

Everything else is just
a glimmer of hope,
held for brief moment
by the click
of the dream sticks.
click.
click.
click.
click.

A Blind Man's Rush Into the Sky

A BLIND MAN'S RUSH
INTO THE SKY

F reedom, at the cost of sanity.
It was like hearing the wind
for the first time.

Eternity opened its door
and the dreamer stepped through,
disappearing, forever
into the silence and agony.
If he made any mistakes in life,
he would have to face them there,
and destroy them.
Before they hunted him down
and forced him from the sky.

He was the ultimate hope
of mankind's battle with fear.
He was pure freedom,
with no responsibilities...
An angel on fire,
riding a black bird
across a nightmare sky...
Alone,
never waking,
never sleeping.

He was a distant star
clinging to old masters.
Living forever
in a world of white light.
In a pitch black dream.

The Danger of Power

THE DANGER OF POWER

When man first looked upon
the land,
he was blinded by what he saw.
He quickly retreated into himself,
back into his cave.

The images he saw were incomprehensible.
Leaving him feeling small,
insignificant.
His despair and pain
echoing forever, as his future,
and his past.
It became a stone around his neck,
a mirror image
of himself.
A painting on the rock wall.

Man's first glimpse of his painted image
conceived for him, a divine pathway,
an escape from the light outside
the cave,
from the fear inside his heart.
This was indeed an omen.
A gift from 'God'.
A pathway of power.
His fear left him
as night became day.

He would follow the man on the wall.

With new strength,
he picked up his weapons
and stepped out
into the sun.

Life on the Moon

LIFE ON THE MOON

A man, trapped in life
sold all he owned
for a brief moment...
a once in a lifetime chance
to see beyond his death...
to dance with it;
and live to tell about it,
as though it was to-day.
It was a dangerous idea
with enormous responsibilities
but he was not allowed pity
or compassion
as a partner in his plan.

I watched the man, trapped in life,
a fool in a glass jar,
his face pressed up against the side,
like a child's face
against a toy store window.
Totally unaware of his existence,
unaware of his shaking hands;
of the cold glass.

Soon the wind from the moon will come
and drive the man away.
Leaving his glass jar behind,
empty and broken.

I am a shadow on the moon
and must stay here,
waiting for the spring,
waiting for the wind to return.

Living Inside a Child's Dream

LIVING INSIDE
A CHILD'S DREAM

F ar out in deep space
sleeps a child.
His face shows no sign of sadness
or pain,
loneliness or cold.

He belongs to no one
and waits for no one.

I have heard people claim
to have seen him
as a man,
waiting at the edge of town.
Others say the child was here once,
but only for a brief moment,
as a child.
I once saw him
as a shadow,
moving quickly through the grass,
racing ahead of a thunderstorm,
avoiding the river...
waiting for nightfall.

Far out in deep space
is a secret.
A tiny chance of hope.
A small child,
asleep.

CHILDREN OF FIRE

I will throw a ball of fire
across the universe,
burning away the stars.
Listen to the insane
when insanity
is the only place left to hide.
Listen to the children
when children
are chosen second
to gold.

I will throw a ball of fire
across the universe
burning away her tears.

The Witness

THE WITNESS

S uddenly the King realized he had
destroyed the wall he built
to protect himself from the night.
Gone was his reflection.
Gone was the wall.
Gone was his image of immortality.
Before him, the pitch black of night
sat waiting, old and rolling
like a living spider's web,
slowly surrounding his throne.

The King, his body shaking,
his insides suddenly empty,
rushed, screaming, into the black nothing.
Alone, without his gold
or identity.
He disappeared forever.

The witness watched this from a high place.
He once told the King, what lay
outside the wall.
No one listened.
Now the witness is alone again.
Watching.
Listening.

NEW WORLD ORDER

I see men crumbling, grumbling,
alone,
and women
no longer crying.
I see children, cold
and indifferent.
I feel a new wind blowing.
It has yellow eyes.

The world around me
is slowly being blown away,
piece by piece.
There is nothing left
to buy or sell.
No where to hide.
I smell dust
and cold.
I am going blind.

A Shadow of a Bird

A SHADOW OF A BIRD

A dance of grace
on a rusty steel wire.
A windmill of sorrow
turning her tired arms
around, around.
No one hears or feels
her aching heart.
Only if she stops,
will she be noticed.

She has become a prisoner
in a forest of ghosts.
A sacred bird
rushing through a tunnel
of fear and ice.

The bird waits alone,
old,
with eyes of black hollow glass.
Watching the wind
roll across the night sky,
like bands of coloured shifting sand.
He can feel their hands
of cold steel, groping
and hear their tongues
clicking, like the teeth
of an angry snake...
Eyes of milky hate and greed.

His shadow has become
the last witness
to his life as a bird.

The painter worked hard
on his tapestry,
forgetting his place in history.
Painting day or night
season after season.
Unaware of the noise around him.
Unaware
of the silence
that watched him.

EPILOGUE

As a poet,
I have become a witness
to life.
To my life.
To the movement
that is life.
As a witness
I am a hermit,
apart, watching,
alone with this choice,
riding the moment of life
like a bird,
high above the land,
above the shadows,
gliding silently
in and out of windows,
in the blackness of space.
There is nothing more.
This is my destiny.

Life is the edge of reason,
that is the beginning
of dreams,
and the edge of History
is the freedom
man fears
the most.
There is nothing more.
This is your destiny.

PROPHECY OF MOVEMENT

The Earth
    in her agony,
will roll onto her side
to ease her pain
and kingdoms of men
will disappear forever.